I07722535

DATE DUE

APR 04

BOOKWORMS

Guess Who Swoops

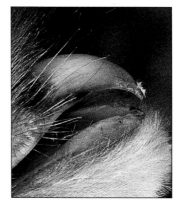

Sharon Gordon

BENCHMARK BOOKS

MARSHALL CAVENDISH

Look up!

Can you see me?

I live in this big, old barn.

No one knows I am here.

I hide my nest and eggs.

I am *nocturnal.*

I get up when the sun goes down.

That is when I hunt for food.

I eat rats, mice, and small birds.

My sharp claws can catch them.

My strong beak can carry them away.

I see in the dark with these small eyes.

My hearing is the best.
I can hear a mouse far,
far away.

I have strong wings.

I can fly quickly.

I can fly quietly.

I swoop down.

I surprise the mouse.

Sometimes, the mouse surprises me!

Screech!

That is all right.

I have all night!

Who am I?

I am an owl!

Who am I?

beak

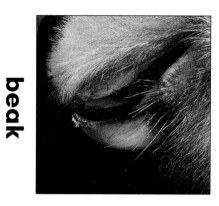

eyes

claws

wings

Challenge Word

nocturnal (nock-ter-nuhl)
A word used to describe an animal that comes out at night.

Index

Page numbers in **boldface** are illustrations.

About the Author

Sharon Gordon has written many books for young children. She has also worked as an editor. Sharon and her husband Bruce have three children, Douglas, Katie, and Laura, and one spoiled pooch, Samantha. They live in Midland Park, New Jersey.

With thanks to Nanci Vargus, Ed.D. and
Beth Walker Gambro, reading consultants

Benchmark Books
Marshall Cavendish
99 White Plains Road
Tarrytown, New York 10591-9001
www.marshallcavendish.com

Text copyright © 2004 by Marshall Cavendish Corporation

Library of Congress Cataloging-in-Publication Data

Gordon, Sharon.
Guess who swoops / by Sharon Gordon.
p. cm. — (Bookworms: Guess who)
Includes index.
Summary: Provides clues about an owl's physical characteristics,
behaviors, and habitats in a guessing game format.
ISBN 0-7614-1553-X
1. Owls—Juvenile literature. [1. Owls.] I. Title.
II. Series: Gordon, Sharon. Bookworms: Guess who.

QL696.S8G67 2003
598.9'7—dc21
2002154567

Photo Research by Anne Burns Images

Cover Photo by: Animals, Animals/Richard Day

The photographs in this book are used with permission and through the courtesy of: Animals, Animals: p. 3 Michael Gadomski;
p. 7 Scott W. Smith; pp. 11, 28 (top right) Stephen Dalton; p. 17 Gerard Lacz. Visuals Unlimited: p. 5 Deneve Feigh Bunde;
pp. 25, 27 Joe McDonald. Peter Arnold: pp. 1, 13, 15, 28 (top left and bottom) Don Riepe; pp. 19, 23, 29 Gerard Lacz;
p. 21 Manfred Danegger. Corbis: p. 9 George Lepp.

Series design by Becky Terhune

Printed in China
1 3 5 6 4 2